ANIMAL PROBLEM-SOLVING

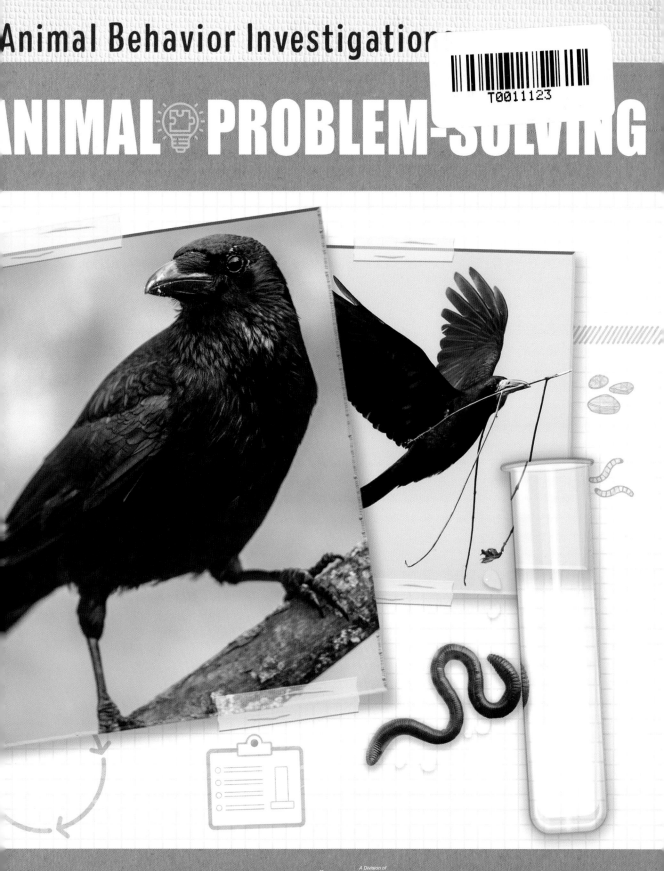

By Michelle Garcia Andersen

Rourke Educational Media

A Division of Carson Dellosa Education

BEFORE AND DURING READING ACTIVITIES

ROURKE'S

SCHOOL to HOME

CONNECTIONS

Before Reading: *Building Background Knowledge and Vocabulary*

Building background knowledge can help children process new information and build upon what they already know. Before reading a book, it is important to tap into what children already know about the topic. This will help them develop their vocabulary and increase their reading comprehension.

Questions and Activities to Build Background Knowledge:

1. Look at the front cover of the book and read the title. What do you think this book will be about?
2. What do you already know about this topic?
3. Take a book walk and skim the pages. Look at the table of contents, photographs, captions, and bold words. Did these text features give you any information or predictions about what you will read in this book?

Vocabulary: *Vocabulary Is Key to Reading Comprehension*

Use the following directions to prompt a conversation about each word.

- Read the vocabulary words.
- What comes to mind when you see each word?
- What do you think each word means?

Vocabulary Words:
- creatures
- hyenas
- insight
- prey
- problem-solve
- researchers
- termites
- tools

During Reading: *Reading for Meaning and Understanding*

To achieve deep comprehension of a book, children are encouraged to use close reading strategies. During reading, it is important to have children stop and make connections. These connections result in deeper analysis and understanding of a book.

Close Reading a Text

During reading, have children stop and talk about the following:

- Any confusing parts
- Any unknown words
- Text to text, text to self, text to world connections
- The main idea in each chapter or heading

Encourage children to use context clues to determine the meaning of any unknown words. These strategies will help children learn to analyze the text more thoroughly as they read.

When you are finished reading this book, turn to the next-to-last page for **Text-Dependent Questions** and an **Extension Activity**.

Table of Contents

The Clever Bird Catches the Worm

Did you know that humans aren't the only creatures who can problem-solve? Animals can solve problems and puzzles too. Researchers wanted to study how rooks solve problems. A rook is a type of crow. Rooks can solve problems in many surprising ways. Researchers wanted to learn more about the ways these birds solve problems.

Rook

The researchers gave the birds tubes of water with worms inside them. They also gave the birds stones. The tubes were only partially filled with water. The researchers saw that the birds were able to get the worms. What do you think the birds did? How did the rooks solve the problem?

What's Their Problem?

Animals problem-solve for many reasons. Some do so because they don't want to quit or give up. They learn from their mistakes. This is called *trial and error*. Even when they fail, they keep trying until they succeed. One example of this is a dog who tries to escape through a fence and doesn't quit until he finds a way.

Huskies

Labrador Retriever

Goal → First Solution → Failure → New Solution → Success → Goal

Learning Through Change

Finding a solution can take several tries. Most of the time, the person or animal will try solutions that do not work before they find one that does. The steps in this process are shown in this diagram.

Animals also solve problems by watching others. They watch other animals or people and copy them. This happened with a macaque (muh-KAK) monkey in Japan. The monkey lived by the sea and ate sweet potatoes. She did not like sand on her sweet potatoes. She washed them in water. She liked to clean her potatoes before she ate them. The other monkeys in her group watched her closely. Soon they also learned to wash their sweet potatoes.

Japanese macaque monkey

Some animals solve problems using insight. That means they have the ability to understand things all of a sudden. Elephants are one example of animals that have insight. Scientists have observed other animals display insight, too. An animal that suddenly stands on a box to reach a tall tree branch has insight.

Finding Solutions

Some animals solve problems to get food. For example, chimpanzees eat **termites** from deep in the ground. It is hard for the chimpanzees to reach their food. They solve this problem by using **tools**. They place sticks and twigs into the holes and pull the bugs out. This is called *termite fishing.*

Chimpanzees

Crows also solve puzzles and use tools to get food. They connect items to make long poles. They use these tools to get food that's out of reach. Crows use what they can to solve problems and get what they want.

Some animals work together to solve problems. Researchers wanted to know if spotted hyenas could work together. Two hyenas had to each pull a rope at the same time. The ropes opened a box above the ground. The box was full of food. The hyenas had no training, but they knew what to do. They pulled the ropes, and the food poured down. They solved the problem in no time!

Spotted Hyenas

Some animals problem-solve to stay safe. One type of octopus uses coconut shells and seashells as tools for safety. This octopus carries the shells around and waits. It hides inside of the shells when it's unsafe. It also uses them to catch prey. The octopus waits for food to come along, and SURPRISE! The octopus pops out and gets a meal.

Coconut Octopus

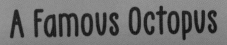

Inky the Octopus

A Famous Octopus

Octopuses can solve puzzles and problems. Inky the octopus was so good at it that he became famous for it. One night, Inky escaped his tank, slithered down a floor drain, and headed out to sea.

The Crow Knows

Now that you know more about animal problem-solving, think about the rooks in the beginning of the book. They needed to reach the worms in the tubes of water. How do you think the crows solved their "worm problem"?

The rooks used the rocks to help them get the food. They dropped the rocks into the tubes of water. The rocks raised the water level. This placed the worms within reach of the rooks. The birds even knew which rocks were best for the job. The bigger the rocks, the fewer the rooks needed to use. These birds are as good at problem-solving as some young children. Now that's pretty amazing!

To learn more about the case study and scientists in this book, search online for "*rook water tube experiment*" and "*Dr. Nathan Emery.*"

Get Creative! Animal Extension Activity

Animals can solve problems in lots of different ways. Humans can do the same thing, but we usually have inventions to help us. You can learn from animals! Design an experiment to test a new, animal-inspired way that you can solve a problem in your life.

1. Brainstorm three small problems that you have and that an animal might also have. For example, you might think about how eating some foods can be messy.

2. Research ways that animals solve these problems or similar ones.

3. Decide what problem-solving method you want to try. Make any necessary adjustments to make it work with your specific problem and the items around you.

4. Test your new problem-solving skill!

Design your study. Make sure it is safe for living things. Write a plan for your study and share it with a friend.

Glossary

creatures (KREE-churz): living beings, human or animal

hyenas (hye-EE-nuhz): wild animals that look somewhat like a dog

insight (IN-site): the ability to understand something that is not obvious

prey (pray): an animal that is hunted by another animal for food

problem-solve (PRAH-bluhm solv): to answer or explain a difficult situation, puzzle, or need

researchers (REE-surch-erz): people who collect and study information about a subject through reading, investigating, or experimenting

termites (TUR-mitez): insects similar to ants that eat wood

tools (toolz): pieces of equipment used to do a particular job (for example, to repair or make things)

Index

Text-Dependent Questions

1. Why is insight important for animal problem-solving?
2. How do chimpanzees get termites out of holes deep in the ground?
3. How do octopuses use coconut shells and seashells?
4. Why do the Japanese macaque monkeys wash their sweet potatoes in water before eating them?
5. What are two kinds of animals that work in a group to problem-solve?

Further Reading

Duling, Kaitlyn. *Hyenas*, Bellwether Media, 2019

Montgomery, Sy. *The Octopus Scientists*, HMH, 2015.

Pringle, Laurence. *Crows!: Strange and Wonderful*, Boyds Mill Press, 2010.

About the Author

Michelle Garcia Andersen lives in southern Oregon. She has three grown kids and lots of pets. Michelle has been very lucky to have raised several dogs in her lifetime, and they are her favorite animal. Her most recent dog, Stella, is a problem-solver. Stella has learned through trial and error how to escape her kennel and run free.

www.rourkeeducationalmedia.com

PHOTO CREDIT: Cover ©Rudmer Zwerver, ©Emi, ©Dorothy.Wedel, ©Valentina Razumova; back cover ©apiguide; p2 ©32 Pixels; p4 ©LFRabanedo; p5 ©FrimuFilms; p5 ©32Pixels; p6 ©Artur Bociarski; p7 ©South_agency; p7 ©32Pixels; p8 DGDimages; p9 ©Aksakalko; p9 ©32Pixels; p10 ©Nature Picture Library; p11 ©GUDKOV ANDREY; p11 ©32Pixels; p12 ©Alexwilco, ©mark Higgins; p13 ©Martin Fowler, ©Sandra Standbridge, ©32Pixels; p14 ©J.NATAYO; p15 ©Cristine Drea; p16 ©David Evison; p17 ©Sascha Janson, ©National Aquarium of New Zealand, ©32Pixels; p18 ©Dr. Sarah Jeibert; p19 ©Sue A Dunning; p20 ©OvidiuAndrei; p21 ©BonD80, ©Boltenkoff, ©IB Photography, ©Hurst Photo, ©Frame Art; p24 ©Michelle Garcia Andersen

Edited by: Tracie Santos
Cover and interior layout by: Tammy Ortner

Library of Congress PCN Data

Animal Problem-Solving / Michelle Garcia Andersen
(Animal Behavior Investigations)
ISBN 978-1-73164-938-6 (hard cover)(alk. paper)
ISBN 978-1-73164-886-0 (soft cover)
ISBN 978-1-73164-990-4 (e-Book)
ISBN 978-1-73165-042-9 (ePub)
Library of Congress Control Number: 2021935285

Rourke Educational Media
Printed in the United States of America
01-1872111937